I grew up in a simpler time, in a
of everything. I wanted the Lion
reflect my lifestyle and values. Va.
are designed for use in making all types of hand-crafted garments,
accessories and home decorating pieces. The yarns have a sophisticated
color palette designed to mix and match, and they have the easy wash-
and-wear care that I love.

When you visit LionBrand.com you'll find the full range of 57 colors of
Vanna's Choice® and 14 colors of Vanna's Glamour™. I also invite you
to join over 140,000 fans of Lion Brand® on Facebook where you'll meet
others who share our love of yarn.

It means a lot to me that the sales of these yarns support St. Jude
Children's Research Hospital, a charity that is close to my heart. In just
three years, Lion Brand® and I have donated over $500,000 to this worthy
cause.

Everything we knit or crochet becomes part of our legacy, so I know how
important it is to use the right yarn. I've taught my daughter, Giovanna,
who is pictured with me on the cover of this book, the craft that I love so
much. She now shares my appreciation for the treasure that a handmade
gift really is.

I hope you find inspiration and ideas from the patterns in this book.
I know the gifts you make will warm the hearts of everyone who receives
them.

*Vanna White*

# 5¹/₂ HOUR THROW

◖■▭▭ **EASY**

## SIZE
About 45 x 60 in. (114.5 x 152.5 cm)

## MATERIALS
LION BRAND® VANNA'S CHOICE® (Art. #860)
    #135 Rust 5 balls (A)
    #133 Brick 5 balls (B)
    or colors of your choice
LION BRAND® VANNA'S GLAMOUR™ (Art. #861)
    #170 Topaz 5 balls (C)
    or color of your choice
LION BRAND® crochet hook size Q-19 (15 mm)
LION BRAND® large-eyed blunt needle

## ADDITIONAL MATERIALS
11 in. (28 cm) piece of cardboard

## GAUGE
About 3 V-sts + 4 rows = 6 in. (15 cm) in pattern with 1 strand each of A, B and C held together.
BE SURE TO CHECK YOUR GAUGE.

## NOTE
Throw is worked with 1 strand each of A, B and C held together.

## THROW
With 1 strand each of A, B and C held together, ch 67.

**Row 1:** Dc in 5th ch from hook, ch 1, dc in same ch (V-st made), *sk 2 ch, (dc, ch 1, dc) in next ch (V-st made); repeat from * to last 2 ch, sk 1 ch, dc in last ch.

**Rows 2-39:** Ch 3, turn, (dc, ch 1, dc) in each ch-1 space across, dc in 3rd ch of turning ch.
Fasten off.

**TIP** Take care not to miss a stitch when working with a large hook.

## FINISHING
### Side Edging
From RS, with 1 strand each of A, B and C held together, work
1 row of single crochet evenly spaced along side edge of Throw. Repeat
on opposite side edge.
Weave in ends.

## Fringe
Wrap A, B and C around cardboard. Cut strands at one end. For each
Fringe, hold 3 strands of each yarn (9 strands total) together and fold
in half. Use crochet hook to draw fold through edge of Throw, forming
a loop. Pull ends of Fringe through this loop and tighten. Make Fringe
along both ends of Throw. Trim Fringe ends evenly.

# POTATO CHIP SCARVES

 **EASY**

## SIZE
Each Scarf measures about 2¼ x 55 in. (5.5 x 139.5 cm)

## MATERIALS
LION BRAND® VANNA'S CHOICE® (Art. #860)

> #141 Wild Berry 1 ball (A)
> #173 Dusty Green 1 ball (B)
> #142 Rose 1 ball (C)
> or colors of your choice

LION BRAND® crochet hook size J-10 (6 mm)
LION BRAND® large-eyed blunt needle

## GAUGE
13 dc + 6 rows = 4 in. (10 cm).
BE SURE TO CHECK YOUR GAUGE.

## SCARVES
(make 3 – 1 each with A, B, and C)
Ch 143.
**Row 1:** Sc in 2nd ch from hook and in each ch across – 142 sc at the end of this row.
**Row 2:** Ch 2 (counts as dc here and throughout), turn, 2 dc in first sc, *dc in next sc, 2 dc in next sc; rep from * across to last sc, dc in last sc – 214 dc at the end of this row.
**Row 3:** Ch 2, turn, 2 dc in first dc, *dc in next dc, 2 dc in next dc; rep from * across to last dc, dc in last dc – 322 dc at the end of this row.
**Row 4:** Ch 2, 2 dc in first dc, *dc in next 2 dc, 2 dc in next dc; rep from * across – 431 dc at end of this row.
Fasten off.

## FINISHING
Weave in ends.

> **TIP** Twist two of your completed scarves together for the two-color effect, or just wear one scarf, like Giovanna.

# GO LIGHTLY TOTE

◆■□□ **EASY +**

## SIZE
About 35 in. (89 cm) circumference at widest point

## MATERIALS
LION BRAND® VANNA'S GLAMOUR™ (Art. #861)
>  #100 Diamond 3 balls (A)
>  #150 Platinum 3 balls (B)
>  or colors of your choice

LION BRAND® crochet hook size I-9 (5.5 mm)
LION BRAND® large-eyed blunt needle

## GAUGE
12 dc = 4 in. (10 cm) over pattern with 1 strand each of A and B held tog.
BE SURE TO CHECK YOUR GAUGE.

## STITCH EXPLANATION
**dc2tog (dc 2 together)** Yo, insert hook in sp between next 2 sts and draw up a loop, yo and draw through all loops on hook – 1 st decreased; yo, insert hook in next sp and draw up a loop, yo and draw through 2 loops; yo and draw through all loops on hook.

## NOTES
1. Work dc into sps between st, rather than into sts.
2. Bag is worked with 1 strand each of A and B held tog throughout.

## BAG
With 1 strand each of A and B held tog, ch 3; join with sl st in first ch to form a ring.

**Rnd 1:** Ch 3 (counts as first dc here and throughout), work 11 more dc in ring; join with sl st in sp between beg ch and next dc – 12 dc.

**Rnd 2:** Ch 3, turn, dc in same sp as join; *2 dc in next sp between sts; rep from * around; join with sl st in sp between beg ch and next dc – 24 dc.

> **TIP** Adjust the length of the handles to suit your needs.

**Rnd 3:** Ch 3, turn, dc in same sp as join, dc in next sp between sts, *2 dc in next sp between sts, dc in next sp between sts; rep from * around; join with sl st in sp between beg ch and next dc – 36 dc.

**Rnd 4:** Ch 3, turn, dc in same sp as join, dc in next 2 sps between sts, *2 dc in next sp between sts, dc in next 2 sps between sts; rep from * around; join with sl st in sp between beg ch and next dc – 48 dc.

**Rnd 5:** Ch 3, turn, dc in same sp as join, dc in next 3 sps between sts, *2 dc in next sp between sts, dc in next 3 sps between sts; rep from * around; join with sl st in sp between beg ch and next dc – 60 dc.

**Rnd 6:** Ch 3, turn, dc in each sp around; join with sl st in sp between beg ch and next dc.

**Rnd 7:** Ch 3, turn, dc in same sp as join, dc in next 4 sps between sts, *2 dc in next sp between sts, dc in next 4 sps between sts; rep from * around; join with sl st in sp between beg ch and next dc – 72 dc.

**Rnd 8:** Ch 3, turn, dc in same sp as join, dc in next 7 sps between sts, *2 dc in next sp between sts, dc in next 7 sps between sts; rep from * around; join with sl st in sp between beg ch and next dc – 81 dc.

**Rnd 9:** Ch 3, turn, dc in same sp as join, dc in next 8 sps between sts, *2 dc in next sp between sts, dc in next 8 sps between sts; rep from * around; join with sl st in sp between beg ch and next dc – 90 dc.

**Rnd 10:** Ch 3, turn, dc in same sp as join, dc in next 9 sps between sts, *2 dc in next sp between sts, dc in next 9 sps between sts; rep from * around; join with sl st in sp between beg ch and next dc – 99 dc.

**Rnds 11–22:** Rep Rnd 6.

**Rnd 23:** Ch 3, turn, dc in next 30 sps between sts, dc2tog, *dc in next 31 sps between sts, dc2tog; rep from * once more; join with sl st in sp between beg ch and next dc – 96 dc.

**Rnd 24:** Rep Rnd 6.

**Rnd 25:** Ch 3, turn, dc in next 29 sps between sts, dc2tog, *dc in next 30 sps between sts, dc2tog; rep from * once more; join with sl st in sp between beg ch and next dc – 93 dc.

**Rnd 26:** Rep Rnd 6.

**Rnd 27:** Ch 3, turn, dc in next 28 sps between sts, dc2tog, *dc in next 29 sps between sts, dc2tog; rep from * once more; join with sl st in sp between beg ch and next dc – 90 dc.

**Rnd 28:** Rep Rnd 6. Do not fasten off.

## Handles
**Row 29:** Ch 3, dc2tog, dc in next 29 sps, dc2tog, dc in next sp; leave remaining sts unworked – 33 sts.

**Rows 30-41:** Ch 3, turn, dc2tog, dc in each sp across to last 3 sps, dc2tog, dc in next sp – 9 sts.

**Rows 42-48:** Ch 3, turn, dc in each sp across – 9 sts. Fasten off at end of Row 48.
Skip 10 sps from last st worked on Row 29. Join 1 strand each of A and B with sl st in next sp, ch 3 and work same as for first handle. Do not fasten off. From wrong side, sc ends of handles tog. Do not fasten off.

## FINISHING
With 1 strand each of A and B held tog, sc evenly around edge of handle. Fasten off.
From right side, join 1 strand each of A and B held tog with sl st at opposite end of handle seam. Sc evenly around edge of handle. Fasten off.
Weave in ends.

# BRIDESMAID PURSE

 **EASY +**

## SIZE
About 4¹/₂ x 10 in. (11.5 x 25.5 cm)

## MATERIALS
LION BRAND® VANNA'S GLAMOUR™ (Art. #861)
   #149 Moonstone 2 balls
   or color of your choice
LION BRAND® crochet hook size F-5 (3.75 mm)
LION BRAND® large-eyed blunt needle

## ADDITIONAL MATERIALS
Sewing needle and thread
One magnetic purse closure

## GAUGE
1 ripple = 3¹/₂ in. (9 cm).
BE SURE TO CHECK YOUR GAUGE.

## PURSE
With A, ch 69.
**Row 1:** Work 2 sc in 2nd ch from hook, sc in each of next 9 ch, sk next 2 ch, *sc in each of next 10 ch, 3 sc in next ch, sc in each of next 10 ch, sk next 2 ch; rep from * once more; sc in each of next 9 ch, 2 sc in last ch – 3 ripples.

**Row 2:** Ch 1, turn, working in back loops only, 2 sc in first st, sc in each of next 9 sts, sk next 2 sts, *sc in each of next 10 sts, 3 sc in next st, sc in each of next 10 sts, sk next 2 sts; rep from * once more; sc in each of next 9 sts, 2 sc in last st. Change to B.
Rep Row 2 until piece measures about 13 in. (33 cm) from beg.

**TIP** Sew a fabric lining inside of purse for added strength.

**Fill-in Ripples**
**Note:** Fill-in Ripples are worked along one side of piece to create a straight edge.

**Row 1:** Ch 1, turn, sk first st, sc in first 9 sts, sk next 2 sts, sc in next 9 sts; leave rem sts unworked.

**Row 2:** Ch 1, turn, sk first st, sc in next 7 sts, sk next 2 sts, sc in next 7 sts; leave rem st unworked.

**Row 3:** Ch 1, turn, sk first st, sc in next 5 sts, sk next 2 sts, sc in next 5 sts; leave rem st unworked.

**Row 4:** Ch 1, turn, sk first st, sc in next 3 sts, sk next 2 sts, sc in next 3 sts; leave rem st unworked.

**Row 5:** Ch 1, turn, sk first st, sc in next st, sk next 2 sts, sc in next st; leave rem st unworked.

**Row 6:** Ch 1, turn, sk first st, sl st in last st.
Fasten off.

**Next Fill-in** Sk next 3-sc group, following previous filled-in ripple. Join yarn with sc in next st, sc in next 8 sc, sk next 2 sc, sc in next 9 sc; leave rem sts unworked. Rep Fill in Rows 2-6. Fasten off. Fill last ripple in same way.

## FINISHING
Fold end with filled-in ripples about 4½ in. (11.5 cm) to form body of Purse. Sew side seams.

**Outside Edging**
From RS, join yarn with sc in top of side seam. Sc evenly around entire outside edge of flap, then sc across straight top edge of Purse. Join with sl st in beg sc. Fasten off.
With sewing needle and thread, sew one half of magnetic closure to inside of flap and the other half to front of Purse. Weave in ends.

# EVENING ALLURE CAPE

●■■◻ **INTERMEDIATE**

## SIZE
**Length** 17 in. (43 cm)
**Width at Lower Edge** 58 in. (147.5 cm)

## MATERIALS
LION BRAND® VANNA'S GLAMOUR™ (Art. #861)
      #150 Platinum 2 balls (A)
      or color of your choice
LION BRAND® VANNA'S CHOICE® (Art. #860)
      #099 Linen 2 balls (B)
      or color of your choice
LION BRAND® crochet hook size N-13 (9 mm)
LION BRAND® large-eyed blunt needle

## ADDITIONAL MATERIALS
One button, ¾ in. (19 mm) diameter

## GAUGE
8 sc = 4 in. (10 cm); 4 rows = 4 in. (10 cm) in pattern with 1 strand each of A and B held tog.
BE SURE TO CHECK YOUR GAUGE.

## NOTE
Shawl is worked with 1 strand each of A and B held tog throughout.

## STITCH EXPLANATION
**dc2tog (dc 2 together)** Yarn over, insert hook in indicated st and draw up a loop, yarn over and draw through 2 loops. Yarn over, insert hook into next indicated st and draw up a loop. Yarn over, draw through 2 loops, yarn over and draw through all loops on hook – 1 st decreased.

> **TIP** If desired, you can replace the button and button loop by simply using a pretty shawl pin.

## SHAWL

With 1 strand each of A and B held tog, ch 66.

**Row 1 (RS):** Sc in 2nd ch from hook and each ch across – 65 sc.

**Row 2:** Ch 7, turn, sk first 2 sc, sc in next sc, (ch 5, sk next 3 sc, sc in next sc) 15 times, ch 3, sk next sc, tr in last sc – 15 ch-5 sps.

**Row 3:** Ch 1, turn, sc in first tr, sk first ch-3 sp, (ch 5, sc in next ch-5 sp, ch 3, 7 tr in next ch-5 sp, ch 3, sc in next ch-5 sp) 5 times, ch 5, sc in 4th ch of beg ch – five 7-tr groups.

**Row 4:** Ch 7, turn, sc in first ch-5 sp, (ch 5, sk next ch-3 sp, sk next tr, sc in next tr, ch 5, sk next 3 tr, sc in next tr, ch 5, sk next tr, sk next ch-3 sp, sc in next ch-5 sp) 5 times, ch 3, tr in last sc.

**Row 5:** Rep Row 3.

**Row 6:** Ch 7, turn, sc in first ch-5 sp, *ch 3, sk next ch-3 sp, tr in next tr, (ch 1, tr in next tr) 6 times, ch 3, sk next ch-3 sp, sc in next ch-5 sp; rep from * 4 more times, ch 3, tr in last sc.

**Row 7:** Ch 1, turn, sc in first tr, *ch 5, sk next 2 ch-sps, sc in next tr, (ch 5, sk next tr, sc in next tr) 3 times; rep from * 4 more times, ch 5, sc in 4th ch of beg ch.

**Row 8:** Ch 7, turn, sc in first ch-5 sp, (ch 5, sc in next ch-5 sp, ch 3, 7 tr in next ch-5 sp, ch 3, sc in next ch-5 sp, ch 5, sc in next ch-5 sp) 5 times, ch 3, tr in last sc.

**Row 9:** Ch 1, turn, sc in first tr, sk first ch-3 sp, *ch 5, sc in next ch-5 sp, ch 3, sk next ch-3 sp, tr in next tr, (ch 1, tr in next tr) 6 times, ch 3, sk next ch-3 sp, sc in next ch-5 sp; rep from * 4 more times, ch 5, sc in 4th ch of beg ch.

**Row 10:** Ch 7, turn, sc in first ch-5 sp, *ch 5, sk next ch-3 sp, sk next tr, (dc2tog over next ch-1 sp and next tr, ch 3) 5 times, dc2tog over next ch-1 sp and next tr, ch 5, sk next ch-3 sp, sc in next ch-5 sp; rep from * 4 more times, ch 3, tr in last sc.

**Row 11:** Ch 1, turn, sc in first tr, sk first ch-3 sp, *ch 5, sc in next ch-5 sp, (ch 5, sk next ch-3 sp, sc in next ch-3 sp) twice, ch 5, sk next ch-3 sp, sc in next ch-5 sp; rep from * 4 more times, ch 5, sc in 4th ch of beg ch.

**Rows 12–14:** Rep Rows 8–10.

**Row 15:** Ch 1, turn, sc in first tr, sk first ch-3 sp, (ch 5, sc in next ch-5 sp, ch 5, sk next ch-3 sp, sc in next ch-3 sp, ch 3, 7 tr in next ch-3 sp, ch 3, sc in next ch-3 sp, ch 5, sk next ch-3 sp, sc in next ch-5 sp) 5 times, ch 5, sc in 4th ch of beg ch.

**Row 16:** Ch 7, turn, sc in first ch-5 sp, *ch 5, sc in next ch-5 sp, ch 3, sk next ch-3 sp, tr in next tr, (ch 1, tr in next tr) 6 times, ch 3, sk next ch-3 sp, sc in next ch-5 sp, ch 5, sc in next ch-5 sp; rep from * 4 more times, ch 3, tr in last sc.

**Row 17:** Ch 1, turn, sc in first tr, sk first ch-3 sp, *ch 5, sc in next ch-5 sp, ch 5, sk next ch-3 sp, sk next tr, (dc2tog over next ch-1 sp and next tr, ch 3) 5 times, dc2tog over next ch-1 sp and next tr, ch 5, sk next ch-3 sp, sc in next ch-5 sp; rep from * 4 more times, ch 5, sc in 4th ch of beg ch.

## Edging

**Rnd 18 (RS):** Ch 1, do not turn; working along side edge, work 3 sc in end of each tr row and 1 sc in end of each sc row to top edge, working 3 sc in corner (end of last sc row); working along opposite side of foundation ch, work sc in each st across top to last st, 3 sc in last st; working along opposite side edge, work 3 sc in end of each tr row and 1 sc in end of each sc row to lower edge, working 3 sc in corner (end of last sc row); working along lower edge (each ch, sc, and dc2tog count as one st), ch 5, sl st in 2nd ch from hook, (sk next st, dc in next st, ch 2, sl st in 2nd ch from hook (picot made)) twice, *sk next 3 sts, (dc in next st, picot, sk next st) 14 times, dc in next st, picot, sk next 3 sts, dc in next st, picot, sk next st, dc in next st, picot; rep from * across to last 3 sts, sk next st, dc in next st; join with sl st in first sc.

**Row 19 (button loop):** Ch 1, sc in each sc up side edge, across top edge, and down opposite side edge, work button loop at top right neck edge as follows: (ch 1, sk next st, sc in next st); at end of last side edge join with sl st in 3rd ch of beg ch-5 of lower edge. Fasten off.

## FINISHING

Sew button opposite button loop. Weave in ends.

# NATURALLY NEUTRAL VEST

■■■◗ **INTERMEDIATE**

## SIZES

S (M, L, 1X, 2X)
**Finished Bust** 36 (38, 42$^{1}/_{2}$, 46, 50) in. (91.5 (96.5, 108, 117, 127) cm), closed.
**Finished Length** 27 (27$^{1}/_{2}$, 28, 28$^{1}/_{2}$, 29$^{1}/_{2}$) in. (68.5 (70, 71, 72.5, 75) cm), including lower band
**Note** Pattern is written for smallest size with changes for larger sizes in parentheses. When only one number is given, it applies to all sizes. To follow pattern more easily, circle all numbers pertaining to your size before beginning.

## MATERIALS

LION BRAND® VANNA'S CHOICE® (Art. #860)
      #153 Black 3 (4, 4, 5, 5) balls (A)
      #126 Chocolate 2 (2, 3, 3, 4) balls (B)
      #099 Linen 2 (4, 4, 6, 6) balls (C)
      or colors of your choice
LION BRAND® circular knitting needle size 8 (5 mm), 29 in. (73.5 cm) long
LION BRAND® knitting needles size 8 (5 mm)
LION BRAND® knitting needles size 9 (5.5 mm)
LION BRAND® large-eyed blunt needle

## GAUGE

15 sts + 21 rows = 4 in. (10 cm) in St st (k on RS, p on WS), with larger needles.
BE SURE TO CHECK YOUR GAUGE.

## NOTES

1. Back is worked from lower edge upwards. Fronts are worked from side to side, from the center front toward the side edge.
2. The Center Front Garter st bands at beg of both fronts are decreased at both ends. The shaped edges of these bands are sewn tog later with the shaped edges of the lower band and neckband.

**TIP**    For ease in counting Garter st rows: 1 ridge = 2 rows.

Naturally Neutral Vest | 17

## STITCH EXPLANATIONS

**kfb (knit into front and back)** Knit next st without removing it from left needle, then k through back of the same st – 1 st increased.

**pbf (purl into back and front)** Purl through back of next st without removing it from left needle, then p through front of same st – 1 st increased.

**skp** Slip 1 st as if to knit, knit 1, pass slip stitch over knit stitch – 1 st decreased.

**ssp (slip, slip, purl)** Slip next 2 sts as if to knit, one at a time, to right needle; slip them back to left needle; purl them together through back loops – 1 st decreased.

## STRIPE SEQUENCE

Work in St st (k on RS, p on WS), *10 rows with B, 14 rows with C, 6 rows with A, 10 rows with B, 6 rows with A, 14 rows with C, 8 rows with A; rep from * for Stripe Sequence.

## RIGHT FRONT
### Garter St Band

With smaller needles and A, cast on 72 sts.

**Row 1 (RS):** Knit.

**Row 2:** Skp, knit across to last 2 sts, k2tog – 70 sts at the end of this row.
Rep last 2 rows 6 more times – 58 sts when all reps have been completed.

### Striped Body

Change to larger needles and B. Beg working in Stripe Sequence.

**Row 1 (RS):** Knit.

**Row 2:** Purl across to last 2 sts, pbf, p1 – 59 sts at the end of this row.
Working in Stripe Sequence as established, rep last 2 rows 12 (14, 16, 18, 20) more times – 71 (73, 75, 77, 79) sts when all reps completed.

**Next Row (RS):** Kfb, knit to end – 72 (74, 76, 78, 80) sts at the end of this row.

**Next Row:** Purl across to last 2 sts, pbf, p1 – 73 (75, 77, 79, 81) sts at the end of this row.
Rep last 2 rows 12 more times – 97 (99, 101, 103, 105) sts when all reps have been completed.

## Shape Shoulder

**Row 1 (RS):** K2, skp, knit to end – 96 (98, 100, 102, 104) sts.

**Row 2:** Purl across to last 4 sts, ssp, p2 – 95 (97, 99, 101, 103) sts.
Rep last 2 rows 6 more times – 83 (85, 87, 89, 91) sts when all reps have been completed.

## Shape Armhole

**Row 1 (RS):** Bind off 25 (26, 27, 28, 29) sts, knit to end – 58 (59, 60, 61, 62) sts.

**Row 2:** Purl.

**Row 3:** K1, skp, knit to end – 57 (58, 59, 60, 61) sts.
Rep last 2 rows 3 (4, 5, 6, 7) more times – 54 sts when all reps have been completed.

**Next Row:** Purl.

**Next Row:** Knit.
Bind off.

## LEFT FRONT
## Garter St Band

With smaller needles and A, cast on 72 sts.

**Row 1 (RS):** Knit.

**Row 2:** Skp, knit across to last 2 sts, k2tog – 70 sts at the end of this row.
Rep last 2 rows 6 more times – 58 sts when all reps have been completed.

## Striped Body

Change to larger needles and B. Beg working in Stripe Sequence.

**Row 1 (RS):** Knit.

**Row 2:** Pbf, purl to end – 59 sts at the end of this row.
Working in Stripe Sequence as established, rep last 2 rows 12 (14, 16, 18, 20) times – 71 (73, 75, 77, 79) sts when all reps have been completed.

**Next Row (RS):** K across to last 2 sts, kfb, k1 – 72 (74, 76, 78, 80) sts.

**Next Row:** Pbf, purl to end – 73 (75, 77, 79, 81) sts.
Rep last 2 rows 12 more times – 97 (99, 101, 103, 105) sts when all reps have been completed.

## Shape Shoulder
**Row 1 (RS):** Knit across to last 2 sts, k2tog, k2 – 96 (98, 100, 102, 104) sts.

**Row 2:** P2, p2tog, purl to end – 95 (97, 99, 101, 103) sts at the end of this row.
Rep last 2 rows 6 more times – 83 (85, 87, 89, 91) sts when all reps have been completed.

## Shape Armhole
**Row 1 (RS):** Knit across to last 25 (26, 27, 28, 29) sts, bind off last 25 (26, 27, 28, 29) sts – 58 (59, 60, 61 62) sts.
Rejoin yarn to work next (WS) row.

**Row 2:** Purl.

**Row 3:** Knit across to last 3 sts, k2tog, k1 – 57 (58, 59, 60, 61) sts.
Rep last 2 rows 3 (4, 5, 6, 7) more times – 54 sts when all reps completed.

**Next Row:** Purl.

**Next Row:** Knit.
Bind off.

## BACK
**Note:** Back begins at lower edge, lower Garter st band will be added later.
With larger needles and B, cast on 76 (80, 88, 94, 102) sts.
Beg working in Stripe Sequence.

**Row 1 (RS):** Knit.

**Row 2:** Purl.

**Rows 3-18:** Rep last 2 rows 8 more times.

**Row 19 (RS):** K1, skp, knit across to last 3 sts, k2tog, k1 – 74 (78, 86, 92, 100) sts at the end of this row.
Rep Rows 2-19, 3 more times – 68 (72, 80, 86, 94) sts when all reps completed.

Work even in St st (k on RS, p on WS) and Stripe Sequence until piece measures 14½ in. (37 cm), end with a WS row.

## Shape Armholes
**Row 1 (RS):** Bind off 4 (4, 5, 5, 6) sts, knit to end – 64 (68, 75, 81, 88) sts at the end of this row.

**Row 2:** Bind off 4 (4, 5, 5, 6) sts, purl to end – 60 (64, 70, 76, 82) sts at the end of this row.

**Row 3:** Bind off 2 (2, 2, 3, 3) sts, knit to end – 58 (62, 68, 73, 79) sts.

**Row 4:** Bind off 2 (2, 2, 3, 3) sts, purl to end – 56 (60, 66, 70, 76) sts.

**Row 5:** K1, skp, knit across to last 3 sts, k2tog, k1 – 54 (58, 64, 68, 74) sts.

**Row 6:** Purl.
Rep last 2 rows 2 (3, 5, 6, 7) more times – 50 (52, 54, 56, 60) sts when all reps completed.
Work even in St st and Stripe Sequence until armhole measures 8 (8½, 9, 9½, 10) in. (20.5 (21.5, 23, 24, 25.5) cm), end with a WS row.

## Shape Shoulders
**Row 1 (RS):** K2, skp, knit across to last 4 sts, k2tog, k2 – 48 (51, 53, 54, 58) sts at the end of this row.

**Row 2:** P2, p2tog, purl to last 4 sts, ssp, p2 – 46 (49, 51, 52, 56) sts.
Rep last 2 rows 6 more times – 22 (25, 27, 28, 32) sts.
Bind off.

## FINISHING
Sew shoulder seams.

**Note:** Circular needle is used to accommodate large number of sts in bands. Work back and forth on circular needle as if working on straight needles.

## Armhole Edging

With RS facing, circular needle and B, pick up and k64 (68, 72, 76, 80) sts evenly spaced along armhole edge.

**Row 1 (WS):** Knit. Change to A.

**Row 2:** With A, purl.
From WS, bind off as if to knit.
Sew side seams, including armhole edging.

## Neckband

With RS facing, circular needle and A, beg inside Garter st band of right front, pick up and k44 (46, 48, 51, 54) sts evenly along right front neck, pick up and k22 (24, 26, 28, 32) sts along Back neck, then pick up and k44 (46, 48, 51, 54) sts evenly along left front neck to Garter st band of left front – 110 (116, 122, 130, 140) sts.

**Row 1 (WS):** K1, kfb, knit across to last 2 sts, kfb, k1 – 112 (118, 124, 132, 142) sts.

**Row 2:** Knit.
Rep last 2 rows 5 more times, then rep Row 1 once more – 124 (130, 136, 144, 154) sts.
Bind off.

## Lower Band

With RS facing, circular needle and A, beg inside Garter st band of left front, pick up and k182 (190, 198, 214, 232) sts evenly spaced along lower edge to Garter st band of Right Front.

**Row 1 (WS):** K1, kfb, knit across to last 2 sts, kfb, k1 – 184 (192, 200, 216, 234) sts.

**Row 2:** Knit.
Rep last 2 rows 5 more times, then rep Row 1 once more – 196 (204, 212, 228, 246) sts.
Bind off.

Sew shaped ends of front bands, neckband and lower band tog. Weave in ends.

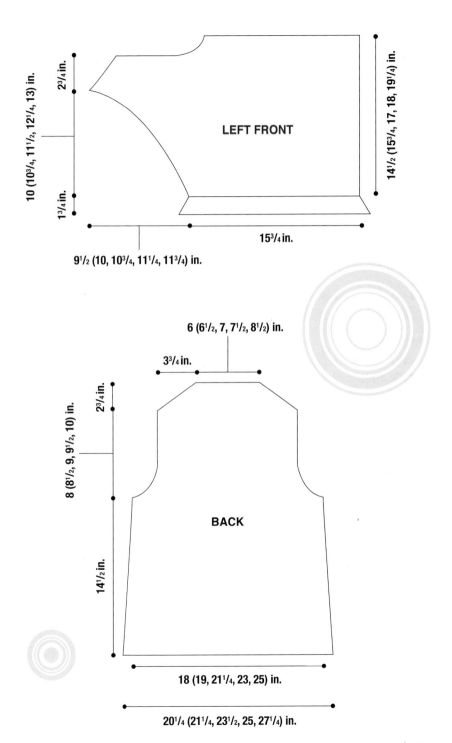

**LEFT FRONT**

10 (10³/₄, 11¹/₂, 12¹/₄, 13) in.

2³/₄ in.

1³/₄ in.

14¹/₂ (15³/₄, 17, 18, 19¹/₄) in.

15³/₄ in.

9¹/₂ (10, 10³/₄, 11¹/₄, 11³/₄) in.

6 (6¹/₂, 7, 7¹/₂, 8¹/₂) in.

3³/₄ in.

**BACK**

2³/₄ in.

8 (8¹/₂, 9, 9¹/₂, 10) in.

14¹/₂ in.

18 (19, 21¹/₄, 23, 25) in.

20¹/₄ (21¹/₄, 23¹/₂, 25, 27¹/₄) in.

# GLITTER SHRUG

◼◼◻◻ **EASY +**

## SIZE
One Size
About 36 x 26 in. (91.5 x 66 cm), before folding and seaming

## MATERIALS
LION BRAND® VANNA'S GLAMOUR™ (Art. #861)
    #170 Topaz 6 balls
    or color of your choice
LION BRAND® stitch markers
LION BRAND® large-eyed blunt needle

## ADDITIONAL MATERIALS
Circular knitting needle size 5 (3.75 mm), 29 in. (73.5 cm) long

## GAUGE
24 sts = 4 in. (10 cm) in St st (k on RS, p on WS).
BE SURE TO CHECK YOUR GAUGE.

## PATTERN STITCH
**K1, p1 Rib (over even number of sts)**
**Row 1:** *K1, p1; rep from * across.
**Row 2:** K the knit sts and p the purl sts.
Rep Row 2 for K1, p1 Rib.

## NOTE
Circular needle is used to accommodate the large number of sts. Work back and forth on circular needle as if working on straight needles.

## SHRUG
Cast on 216 sts.
Work in K1, p1 Rib until piece measures 2 in. (5 cm) from beg.
Change to St st (k on RS, p on WS) and work until piece measures 24 in. (61 cm) from beg.
Work in K1, p1 Rib until piece measures 26 in. (66 cm) from beg.
Bind off.

> **TIP** Use a 29" or longer circular needle to make this shrug.

## FINISHING

Fold piece in half, bringing cast-on and bound-off edges together, to measure 36 x 13 in. (91.5 x 33 cm). Place markers on each of the 13 in. (33 cm) sides, 7 in. (18 cm) below fold for armholes. Seam each side from marker down to lower edge. Weave in ends.

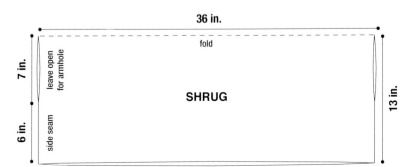

36 in.

fold

7 in.

6 in.

leave open for armhole

side seam

**SHRUG**

13 in.

# HARVEST RIPPLE AFGHAN

 **EASY**

## SIZE
About 42 x 52 in. (106.5 x 132 cm)

## MATERIALS
LION BRAND® VANNA'S CHOICE® (Art. #860)

    #125 Taupe 4 balls (A)
    #130 Honey 2 balls (B)
    #173 Dusty Green 2 balls (C)
    #099 Linen 3 balls (D)
    #147 Purple 2 balls (E)
    or colors of your choice

LION BRAND® crochet hook size J-10 (6 mm)
LION BRAND® large-eyed blunt needle

## GAUGE
1 ripple = about 4¹/₂ in. (11.5 cm).
BE SURE TO CHECK YOUR GAUGE.

## STITCH EXPLANATION
**dc2tog (dc 2 sts together)** Yarn over, insert hook into st and draw up a loop, yarn over and draw through 2 loops. Yarn over, insert hook into next st and draw up a loop. Yarn over, draw through 2 loops, yarn over and draw through all loops on hook – 1 st decreased.

## COLOR SEQUENCE
Work 2 rows of each color in the following Color Sequence: A, B, A, C, D, C, E, A, E, B, D, B, A, C, A, D, E, D.

**Note:** To change color, work last st of old color to last yarn over; yarn over with new color and draw through all loops on hook to complete the st.

> **TIP**   Make this afghan in Vanna's Choice® colors that match your home décor.

## AFGHAN
With A, ch 168.

**Row 1:** Dc in 4th ch from hook (beginning ch counts as dc), (dc2tog) 3 times, 2 dc in next 6 ch, *(dc2tog) 6 times, 2 dc in next 6 ch; rep from * across to last 8 ch, (dc2tog) 3 times, dc in last 2 ch – 9 ripples.

**Row 2:** Ch 3 (counts as first dc), turn, dc in next dc, (dc2tog) 3 times, 2 dc in next 6 dc, *(dc2tog) 6 times, 2 dc in next 6 dc; rep from * across to last 8 dc, (dc2tog) 3 times, dc in last 2 dc. Change to B.
Rep Row 2, continue to change colors every other row following Color Sequence, until Color Sequence has been completed twice.  Fasten off.

## FINISHING
Weave in ends.

# EYELET STRIPS AFGHAN

◖◼◻◻ **EASY**

## SIZE
About 36 x 56 in. (91.5 x 142 cm)

## MATERIALS
LION BRAND® VANNA'S CHOICE® (Art. #860)
> #130 Honey 2 balls (A)
> #144 Magenta 1 ball (B)
> #108 Dusty Blue 1 ball (C)
> #148 Burgundy 1 ball (D)
> #133 Brick 1 ball (E)
> #123 Beige 1 ball (F)
> #158 Mustard 1 ball (G)
> #135 Rust 1 ball (H)
> or colors of your choice

LION BRAND® crochet hook size J-10 (6 mm)
LION BRAND® large-eyed blunt needle

## GAUGE
12 dc + 7 rows = 4 in. (10 cm).
BE SURE TO CHECK YOUR GAUGE.

## FIRST STRIP
With A, ch 174.

**Row 1 (WS):** Dc in 4th ch from hook (beginning ch counts as dc) and in each ch across – 172 dc at end of this row.

**Rows 2 and 3:** Ch 3 (counts as first dc here and throughout), turn, dc in each st across.

**Row 4:** Ch 3, turn, dc in next 3 sts, *ch 2, sk next 2 sts, dc in next 4 sts; rep from * across – 28 ch-2 sps at end of this row.

> **TIP** Make 2 small swatches, then practice your joining row.

**Rows 5-7:** Rep Row 2.
Fasten off.

## SECOND STRIP
**Notes:** Second-Eighth Strips are worked as for First Strip through Row 7, and then joined to previous Strip with a Joining Row. The Joining Row is worked back and forth between the last row of the current strip and the foundation ch of the previous strip.
With B, ch 174.

**Rows 1-7:** Work Rows 1-7 of First Strip. Do not fasten off.
With RS facing, place previous Strip above current Strip.

**Joining Row:** Ch 1, turn, sc in first st of current Strip, ch 2, sc in first foundation ch of previous Strip, ch 3, sk next 2 sts of current Strip, *sc in next st of current Strip, ch 3, sk next 3 sts of previous Strip, sc in next st of previous Strip, ch 3, sk next 3 sts of current Strip; rep across continuing to work back and forth between the 2 Strips, ending with sc in last st of current Strip, ch 2, sk next 2 sts of previous Strip, sc in last st of previous Strip. Fasten off.

## THIRD-EIGHTH STRIPS
With C, D, E, F, G, and H, work as for Second Strip.

## FINISHING
### Edging
With RS facing, join A with sl st in any corner.

**Rnd 1:** Ch 1, sc evenly around outside edge, working 3 sc in each corner; join with sl st in first sc.

**Rnd 2:** Ch 1, sc in each sc around, working 3 sc in each corner; join with sl st in first sc.
Fasten off. Weave in ends.

# ABBREVIATIONS

**beg** = begin(ning)

**ch** = chain

**ch-sp** = chain space previously made

**dc** = double crochet

**hdc** = half double crochet

**inc** = increase

**k** = knit

**k2tog** = knit 2 together

**p** = purl

**p2tog** = purl 2 together

**rem** = remain(s)(ing)

**rep** = repeat

**rnd** = round

**RS** = right side

**sc** = single crochet

**sk** = skip

**sl st** = slip stitch

**sp(s)** = space(s)

**St st** = stockinette stitch

**st(s)** = stitch(es)

**tog** = together

**tr** = triple (treble) crochet

**WS** = wrong side

**yo** = yarn over

Lion Brand Yarn Company® is America's oldest hand knitting yarn brand. Founded in 1878, Lion Brand Yarn Company® is the leading supplier of quality hand knitting and crochet yarns. Throughout its history, Lion Brand Yarn® has been at the forefront of yarn trends while consistently providing its customers with the highest quality product at a value price. The company's mission is to provide ideas, inspiration and education to yarn crafters.